DUTCH OVEN

CAMP COOKING

DUTCH OVEN

OVEN

CAMP COOKING

VERNON WINTERTON

GIBBS SMITH
TO ENRICH AND INSPIRE HUMANKIND

First Edition
26 25 24 23 22   5 4 3 2 1

Text © 2018, 2022 Vernon Winterton
Photographs © 2018, 2022 Susan Barnson Hayward

The content in this book was originally published as *Let's Go Dutch* in 2018
by Gibbs Smith.

Published by
Gibbs Smith
P.O. Box 667
Layton, Utah 84041

1.800.835.4993 orders
www.gibbs-smith.com

Designed by Sheryl Dickert
Food styling by Marcela Ferrinha and Corrine Miller
Printed and bound in China

Gibbs Smith books are printed on either recycled, 100% post-consumer waste,
FSC-certified papers or on paper produced from sustainable PEFC-certified
forest/controlled wood source. Learn more at www.pefc.org.

Library of Congress Cataloging-in-Publication Data

Names: Winterton, Vernon, author. | Hayward, Susan Barnson, photographer.
Title: Dutch oven camp cooking / Vernon Winterton; photographs by Susan
Barnson Hayward.
Description: Layton: Gibbs Smith, [2022] | Includes index.
Identifiers: LCCN 2021036659 | ISBN 9781423661252 (hardcover) | ISBN
9781423661269 (epub)
Subjects: LCSH: Dutch oven cooking. | LCGFT: Cookbooks.
Classification: LCC TX840.D88 W563 2022 | DDC 641.5/89—dc23
LC record available at https://lccn.loc.gov/2021036659

CONTENTS

HELPFUL HINTS

1. When purchasing a Dutch oven, look for lumps in the casting. Lumps cause hot spots you want to avoid. Look at the thickness of all sides of a Dutch oven. If one side is thinner than the other, it will not cook evenly and your results will be poor. Also, make sure the lid sits flat and does not rock to ensure there is a good seal when cooking. However, if the lid moves side to side slightly, that is fine.

2. The Camp Chef Ultimate Dutch Oven, no longer produced by this company, is a special Dutch oven designed for convection cooking, and was made in either aluminum or cast iron. It has a center cone and two racks, one on the bottom for cooking meat and one near the top for cooking vegetables. This oven has many other uses, such as cooking pies and cakes. I use the Camp Chef Ultimate for the Chocolate Cake recipe (page 117) because it is such a moist cake that it does not get done in the middle and burns on the edges when cooked in a regular Dutch oven. It comes out more like a Bundt cake.

3. All Dutch ovens come coated with wax to protect them during shipping (unless they have been preseasoned). To season a new Dutch oven, scrub off all the wax and then coat with shortening. Place the Dutch oven, upside down, in a barbecue or an oven (to allow shortening to drip off when heating) and heat to 400 degrees for 30 minutes. This begins to make the nonstick surface for which Dutch ovens are famous. Let the oven cool naturally, and when you can touch it with your hands, place the lid back on the Dutch oven and let it continue to cool. The more you use the oven, the more seasoned or nonstick it will become. Depending on the frequency of use, you may have to season several times a year. If the oven starts to smell rancid, do the whole seasoning process again.

4. When you clean a Dutch oven after it has been seasoned, don't use soap. The soap pulls the seasoning out and you will have to season it again. Use really hot water and a plastic scrubbing pad. Never use anything metal. Metal will scrape away the oven's nonstick surface.

5. Store a Dutch oven with something between the lid and the pot, such as a rolled-up paper towel. This allows air to flow through it during storage and helps keep the oven from becoming rancid. If the oven gives off a funny pungent smell, you know it is rancid and needs to be seasoned again. If you use your oven year-round, it will not become rancid. If your oven becomes rusty, you are not using it often enough. Scrub the rust off with an SOS pad, dry, and then season it again.

6. Use your Dutch oven year-round; just set it up anywhere it will be protected from wind, such as a patio, garage, or even your home oven. Wind carries the heat away, so it is important to be in a wind-free area.

7. Charcoal briquettes, or coals, are used in all of the recipes in this book, and heat control is important for Dutch oven use. Take the size of the oven, such as a 12-inch pot, then double that number to 24. This gives you the number of coals to start with to reach 350 degrees of heat. A 14-inch oven would be 28, a 16-inch would be 32, and so on. Place 10 coals under the Dutch oven and put the rest on top of the lid. Each additional coal placed on the oven adds approximately 20-25 degrees. For baking, put most of the heat on the lid. For frying, put most of the heat on the bottom. You will almost never put a coal in the center of the oven (bottom or lid) as it will make a hot spot and burn food, causing poor results.

8. Be mindful of the size of your coals so your heat doesn't drop. When coals are the size of a quarter, it's time to replace them with new ones.

9. Rotate the Dutch oven every 10 minutes by moving the lid counterclockwise and bottom clockwise. This will help to cook more evenly, especially with cakes and breads.

10. When reducing sauces or liquids in a recipe, place moisture managers between the lid and the Dutch oven or use clothespins to help hold the lid ajar. This allows the moisture to escape.

11. You may use a Dutch oven in your indoor oven. To use a cast iron oven that has legs, just pull the indoor oven rack out far enough that you can turn the legs on your camp oven to fit between the wires on the rack. Then push it back in the indoor oven and begin the cooking process. If you have a Dutch oven that is meant to be used in an indoor oven, there will be no legs. Just place it in the oven and cook at the temperature in the recipe, no coals needed. There are also Dutch ovens that are covered with porcelain that are specifically made for use in your indoor oven. The cooking times should be about the same whether cooking with coals or in your home oven.

12. Experiment with your Dutch oven and get creative with your recipes. You may even want to enter a Dutch oven cook-off. Look at the International Dutch Oven Society website, www.idos.org, for a cook-off near you.

BREAKFASTS
and
SWEET BREADS

CHEESY BREAKFAST CASSEROLE

1 (12-inch) Dutch oven, 24* hot coals plus extra if needed, cooking temperature 350 degrees

MAKES 8 SERVINGS

1 (24-ounce) package frozen shredded hash brown potatoes, thawed

⅓ cup butter, melted

1 cup shredded cheddar cheese

1 cup shredded Swiss cheese

1 cup cooked and cubed ham

6 eggs

½ cup milk

½ teaspoon salt

Finely chopped chives, optional

Warm the Dutch oven over 10 coals, and then cook the potatoes in the butter until they start to brown. Spread the potatoes evenly over the bottom of the oven and sprinkle both cheeses and ham over top.

In a medium bowl, beat the eggs, milk, and salt together until well combined. Pour evenly over the ham, cheese, and potatoes. Cover with lid and bake for 30–35 minutes, or until eggs are set and cheese is bubbling, using 10 coals underneath the oven and 14 coals on top. Sprinkle with chives, if using, and serve.

*Tip: Remember to check the coals and replace any that have become the size of a quarter with a new hot coal.

BREAKFAST ROLLS

1 (12-inch) Dutch oven, 36 hot coals plus extra if needed, cooking temperature 375 degrees

MAKES 16 ROLLS

Cooking spray

Oil, for cooking, plus more as needed

1 heaping cup cooked, crumbled
   bacon pieces

¾ cup chopped fresh mushrooms

3 tablespoons chopped red onion

9 ounces evaporated milk

6 tablespoons butter

½ cup water

4 ½ cups flour

5 ¼ tablespoons sugar

1 ½ teaspoons salt

3 teaspoons active dry yeast

¾ cup shredded medium cheddar cheese

Drizzle a small amount of oil in the bottom of the Dutch oven. Add the bacon, mushrooms, and onion and cook until mushrooms are tender, using 9 coals underneath the oven. Remove the mixture from the Dutch oven and set aside, leaving any remaining oil.

Add the milk and butter to the Dutch oven and heat until butter is melted. Pour into a large mixing bowl and add water. Add the flour, sugar, salt, yeast, cheese, and bacon mixture; mix well, kneading 2–5 minutes. Place dough in a large lightly oiled bowl and turn to coat. Cover with a clean cloth and set in a warm, draft-free area; let rise until double in size.

Punch down dough, divide into 16 even-size pieces, and roll into balls. Place in same Dutch oven that has been prepared with nonstick cooking spray. Cover with lid and let rise until double in size. When rolls have risen, bake for 30–40 minutes, until golden brown, using 9 coals underneath the oven and 15 on top; replace coals as needed.

Tip: If you find it necessary to wipe out the Dutch oven between uses in a recipe, do not use a paper towel, it will leave little bits of paper behind. Lint-free rags are an option, as well as using parchment paper or aluminum foil as a liner.

MOUNTAIN MAN BREAKFAST

1 (12-inch) Dutch oven, 24 hot coals plus extra if needed, cooking temperature 350 degrees

MAKES 20 SERVINGS

1 pound bacon, cut into 1-inch pieces

1 pound ground sausage of choice, crumbled

2 (24-ounce) packages frozen Southern-style hash brown potatoes, thawed

1 (8-ounce) container sour cream

4 eggs, beaten

1 pound shredded sharp cheddar cheese

Brown the bacon and sausage in the Dutch oven, using 10 coals underneath, until cooked through and bacon is starting to crisp. Stir in hash browns. Cover with lid and bake for 25-30 minutes, using 10 coals underneath the oven and 14 coals on top; replace coals as needed.

In a medium bowl, combine the sour cream and eggs until thoroughly mixed. During the last 5 minutes of cooking, carefully remove lid from Dutch oven and pour the egg mixture evenly over hash browns. Replace lid and continue to cook for 5 minutes, or until eggs are set and cooked through. Remove lid, sprinkle cheese over top, replace lid, and let sit for a few minutes until cheese melts.

BREAKFAST PIZZA

1 (14-inch) Dutch oven, 24 hot coals plus extra if needed, cooking temperature 325 degrees

MAKES 8 SERVINGS

1 pound ground sausage of choice

1 green bell pepper, chopped

1 medium onion, chopped

1 (8-ounce) package sliced fresh
mushrooms

3 (8-ounce) cans Grands refrigerator
biscuits or 1 can refrigerator
pizza crust

10 eggs, well beaten

1 medium tomato, chopped

1 (4-ounce) can sliced black olives

½ pound shredded Monterey Jack cheese

½ pound shredded mozzarella cheese

Salsa of choice

Cook and crumble the sausage with bell pepper, onion, and mushrooms in the Dutch oven, using 10 coals underneath, until sausage is cooked through. Drain excess grease, remove sausage mixture, and set aside.

In the same Dutch oven, arrange the biscuits over the bottom; flatten and pinch together to form a solid crust. Spoon sausage mixture over top. Pour the eggs over the sausage mixture and sprinkle evenly with tomato, olives, and cheeses. Cover with the lid and bake for 30 minutes, or until bottom of crust is completely cooked and cheese is bubbling, using 8 coals underneath the oven and 16 coals on top; replace coals as needed. Serve with salsa on the side.

ROYAL BRAID

1 (12-inch) Dutch oven, 24 hot coals, cooking temperature 350 degrees

MAKES 16 SERVINGS

Cooking spray

Oil

2 cups warm water

1 cup plus 3 tablespoons sugar, divided

2 tablespoons plus ½ teaspoon active dry yeast

3 teaspoons salt

3 tablespoons butter, softened

1 cup plus 1 to 2 tablespoons milk, divided

7 ½ cups flour, divided

½ cup butter, melted, divided

½ cup brown sugar

1 tablespoon cinnamon

1 cup powdered sugar

½ teaspoon vanilla extract

½ cup chopped pecans

In a large mixing bowl, combine water, ⅔ cup sugar, and yeast. When foamy, add salt, softened butter, 1 cup milk, and 5 cups flour. Stir until well mixed then add remaining flour, ½ cup at a time. Knead on a lightly floured surface until a soft dough forms. Place dough in a separate bowl that has been lightly oiled and turn to coat. Cover with a clean cloth and set in a warm, draft-free area for about 45 minutes, or until double in size. Punch down dough and roll out on a lightly floured surface into a 10 x 4-inch rectangle. Brush with half the melted butter.

In a small bowl, combine remaining sugar, brown sugar, and cinnamon; sprinkle evenly over top of dough. Fold dough into thirds and then roll out to a 12 x 4-inch rectangle. Divide the dough lengthwise into 3 equal pieces and braid together. Bring ends together and pinch to form a circle. Place in the Dutch oven that has been prepared with nonstick cooking spray. Cover with lid and bake for 45-55 minutes, or until golden brown, using 10 coals underneath the oven and 14 on top. Remove bread from oven to a wire rack and brush with remaining butter; let cool.

In a small bowl, mix together powdered sugar, remaining milk, and vanilla to desired consistency. Drizzle over cooled braid and then sprinkle with pecans.

RAISIN BREAD

1 (10-inch) Dutch oven, 20 hot coals, cooking temperature 350 degrees

MAKES 1 LOAF

Cooking spray

Oil

1 1/2 cups plus 1 tablespoon warm water

4 tablespoons sugar

1 tablespoon active dry yeast

3 3/4 cups flour

3 tablespoons instant nonfat dry milk

2 1/4 teaspoons salt

1 tablespoon cinnamon

3 tablespoons butter, softened

1 1/2 cups raisins

1/2 cup chopped nuts of choice, optional

In a small mixing bowl, combine the water, sugar, and yeast; set aside.

In a large mixing bowl, mix together the flour, dry milk, salt, cinnamon, butter, raisins, and nuts, if using. Add yeast mixture and knead until a soft dough forms. Place in a lightly oiled bowl and turn to coat. Cover with a clean cloth and let rise in a warm, draft-free area for about 45 minutes, or until double in size.

Punch down dough, form into a loaf, and place in the warmed* Dutch oven that has been prepared with nonstick cooking spray. Cover with a clean cloth and let rise in a warm, draft-free area until double in size. Cover with lid and bake for 40 minutes, or until golden brown, using 8 coals underneath the oven and 12 on top.

*Tip: To warm the Dutch oven, you can place it in the sun or use about 4 coals underneath the oven for just a few minutes. Remember, you want it warm, not hot.

CINNAMON ROLLS

1 (14-inch) Dutch oven, 28 hot coals, cooking temperature 350 degrees

MAKES 10 TO 12 ROLLS

Cooking spray

Oil

½ cup sugar

¾ cup warm water

2 tablespoons active dry yeast

1 cup milk

½ cup potato flakes

¾ cup butter, softened, divided

1 teaspoon salt

2 eggs

4 to 4 ½ cups flour, divided

3 teaspoons cinnamon

1 ½ cups brown sugar

1 ½ cups raisins, optional

¾ cup chopped pecans, optional

1 (16-ounce) container vanilla or cream cheese frosting

In a large mixing bowl, combine sugar, water, yeast, and milk; let sit for 5 minutes. Add potato flakes and mix well. Mix in ½ cup butter, salt, eggs, and 2 cups flour; beat until well combined. Add remaining flour to form a soft, elastic dough. Place dough in a lightly oiled bowl, turning to coat. Cover with a clean cloth and let rise in a warm, draft-free area until double in size. Punch down dough and roll out on a lightly floured surface into a 9 x 11-inch rectangle, about ¼ inch thick. Spread with remaining butter and sprinkle evenly with cinnamon, brown sugar, raisins, and pecans, if using.

Beginning with the long side, roll up dough and pinch the edge together to seal. Cut into 10 to 12 even slices using thread or kitchen string. Place dough slices in the Dutch oven that has been prepared with nonstick cooking spray. Cover with a clean cloth and let rise in a warm, draft-free area until double in size. Cover with the lid and bake for 25–30 minutes, or until golden brown, using 12 coals underneath the oven and 16 on top. Frost rolls while still warm.

STICKY BUNS

1 (12-inch) Dutch oven, 24 hot coals, cooking temperature 350 degrees

MAKES 16 BUNS

Cooking spray

1 cup hot milk

1 tablespoon butter

¼ cup warm water

1 tablespoon sugar

1 tablespoon active dry yeast

3 ½ cups flour, divided

¼ teaspoon salt

1 egg, beaten

½ cup butter, melted

1 cup brown sugar

1 (10-ounce) bag chopped pecans

In a small bowl, stir together hot milk and butter until butter melts. In a separate small bowl, combine water, sugar, and yeast; set aside.

In a large mixing bowl, combine half the flour, salt, egg, and milk mixture. Beat for 5 minutes. Mix in yeast mixture and then the remaining flour until well combined. Knead dough on a lightly floured surface for 10 minutes or until dough is elastic. Place in the Dutch oven that has been prepared with nonstick cooking spray. Cover with the lid and set in a warm, draft-free area until double in size.

Remove dough from Dutch oven and roll into a long log, 2 to 3 inches in diameter, on a lightly floured surface. Cut the dough into 16 even-size pieces and roll into balls. Dip balls halfway into melted butter. Coat buttered side of dough balls in brown sugar and then roll in pecans. Sprinkle any remaining sugar and pecans in the bottom of the Dutch oven. Place dough balls, sugar side down, in Dutch oven. Cover with the lid and bake for 35–40 minutes, or until golden brown, using 10 coals underneath the oven and 14 on top. When done, invert sticky buns onto a serving plate. Scrape out any remaining sauce from the Dutch oven and drizzle over top of buns.

Tip: If you need to speed up the rising process, place 3 coals on the lid.

ORANGE-CRANBERRY ROLLS

1 (12-inch) Dutch oven, 24 hot coals, cooking temperature 350 degrees

MAKES 16 ROLLS

Cooking spray

Oil

4 teaspoons active dry yeast

2 cups warm water, divided

7 tablespoons sugar, divided

6 cups flour

4 tablespoons instant nonfat dry milk

2 teaspoons salt

6 tablespoons butter, softened

1 cup dried or thawed frozen cranberries

2 teaspoons orange extract

2 oranges, zested

In a small bowl, combine yeast, 1 cup water, and 4 tablespoons sugar; set aside.

In a large mixing bowl, combine remaining sugar, flour, dry milk, salt, butter, and cranberries. Stir in the yeast mixture, orange extract, and zest. Add remaining water and knead dough until elastic and cranberries are evenly distributed throughout the dough. Place in a lightly oiled bowl and turn to coat. Cover with a clean cloth and let rise in a warm, draft-free area for 30 minutes, or until double in size.

Punch down dough, cut into 16 even-size pieces, and roll into balls. Place in the warmed* Dutch oven that has been prepared with nonstick cooking spray. Cover with a clean cloth and let rise in a warm, draft-free area until double in size. Cover with the lid and bake for 20-30 minutes or until golden brown, using 10 coals underneath the oven and 14 on top.

*Tip: To warm the Dutch oven, you can place it in the sun or use about 4 coals underneath the oven for just a few minutes. Remember, you want it warm, not hot.

APPLE DUMPLING ROLLS

1 (12-inch) Dutch oven, 1 (5-inch) Dutch oven, 30-32 hot coals, cooking temperature 350 degrees

MAKES 12 ROLLS

Cooking spray

2 cups flour

1 teaspoon salt

2 teaspoons baking powder

¾ cup shortening

½ cup milk

3 to 4 Granny Smith apples, peeled and shredded

Cinnamon, for sprinkling

SAUCE

2 cups water

1 cup sugar

1 cup brown sugar

¼ cup butter

¼ teaspoon cinnamon

In a large mixing bowl, combine the flour, salt, and baking powder; cut in shortening until well combined and mixture is the size of peas. Add milk and mix until a soft dough forms. On a lightly floured surface, roll dough out into a 12 x 16-inch rectangle, about ¼ inch thick. Scatter apples evenly over top and sprinkle with cinnamon. Beginning with the longer side, roll up the dough like a jelly roll and cut into 12 even slices using thread or kitchen string. Place in the 12-inch Dutch oven that has been prepared with nonstick cooking spray.

To make the sauce, add the water, sugars, butter, and cinnamon to the 5-inch Dutch oven and heat until melted together and smooth, using 3 coals underneath the oven and 3 around the outside.

Pour the warm sauce around the rolls. Cover with the lid and bake for 30 minutes, using 8 to 10 coals underneath the oven and 16 on top. Serve warm.

CINNAMON PULL-APARTS

1 (12-inch) Dutch oven, 24 hot coals, cooking temperature 350 degrees

MAKES 16 SERVINGS

Cooking spray

2 cups warm water

1/3 cup sugar

2 tablespoons active dry yeast

1/3 cup oil, plus more as needed

1 1/2 teaspoons salt

1 egg

2/3 cup instant nonfat dry milk

5 to 6 cups flour, divided

1/2 cup butter, melted

1 tablespoon cinnamon, or to taste

1 1/2 cups brown sugar

In a large mixing bowl, combine water, sugar, and yeast; set aside for 5 minutes. Add the oil, salt, and egg. In a separate bowl, combine the dry milk with 2 cups flour and add to yeast mixture. Beat until smooth. Add remaining flour, 1 cup at a time, and mix until smooth. Knead dough on a lightly floured surface until elastic, and then place in a lightly oiled bowl and turn to coat. Cover with a clean cloth and let rise until triple in size. Punch down dough, divide into 16 even-size pieces, and roll into balls; dip in melted butter.

In a small bowl, combine cinnamon and brown sugar. Roll balls in cinnamon mixture and then place in a warmed* Dutch oven that has been prepared with nonstick cooking spray. Pour any leftover cinnamon mixture over top. Cover with the lid and bake for 15-20 minutes, or until golden, using 10 coals underneath the oven and 14 on top. When done, loosen edges with knife and remove to wire rack to cool.

*Tip: To warm the Dutch oven, you can place it in the sun or use about 4 coals underneath the oven for just a few minutes. Remember, you want it warm, not hot.

SAVORY BREADS *and* ROLLS

ITALIAN HERB AND CHEESE LOAF

1 (10-inch) Dutch oven, 20 hot coals, cooking temperature 350 degrees

MAKES 12 SERVINGS

Cooking spray

Oil

1 cup plus 1 tablespoon warm water

1 tablespoon sugar

1 ½ teaspoons active dry yeast

2 ¾ cups flour

1 tablespoon instant nonfat dry milk

1 ½ teaspoons salt

¼ cup freshly grated Parmesan or Asiago cheese

2 teaspoons Italian seasoning

2 tablespoons butter, softened

In a small bowl, combine water, sugar, and yeast; set aside.

In a large mixing bowl, mix together the flour, dry milk, salt, cheese, and Italian seasoning. Mix in butter and yeast mixture, and knead until a soft dough forms. Place in a lightly oiled bowl and turn to coat. Cover with a clean cloth and let rise in a warm, draft-free area until double in size. Punch down dough, form into a round loaf, and place in a warmed* Dutch oven that has been prepared with nonstick cooking spray. Cover and let rise until double in size.

Cover with the lid and bake for 40 minutes, or until golden brown, using 8 coals underneath the oven and 12 on top.

*Tip: To warm the Dutch oven, you can place it in the sun or use about 4 coals underneath the oven for just a few minutes. Remember, you want it warm, not hot.

GARLIC BREAD

1 (10-inch) Dutch oven, 20 hot coals, cooking temperature 350 degrees

MAKES 12 SERVINGS

Cooking spray

Oil

1 cup plus 2 tablespoons warm water

1 tablespoon sugar

2 teaspoons active dry yeast

3 cups flour

1 tablespoon instant nonfat dry milk

1 1/2 teaspoons salt

1 tablespoon dried parsley

1 1/2 to 3 teaspoons garlic powder, or to taste

1 tablespoon butter, softened

In a small bowl, combine water, sugar, and yeast; set aside.

In a large mixing bowl, mix together the flour, dry milk, salt, parsley, and garlic powder. Mix in the butter and yeast mixture and knead until a soft dough forms. Place in a lightly oiled bowl and turn to coat. Cover with a clean cloth and let rise in a warm, draft-free area until double in size. Punch down dough, form into a round loaf, and then place in a warmed* Dutch oven that has been prepared with nonstick cooking spray. Cover and let rise until double in size.

Cover with the lid and bake for 40 minutes, or until golden brown, using 8 coals underneath the oven and 12 on top.

Variation: For garlic lovers, try replacing the garlic powder with minced or chopped fresh or dried garlic, to taste.

*Tip: To warm the Dutch oven, you can place it in the sun or use about 4 coals underneath the oven for just a few minutes. Remember, you want it warm, not hot.

EASY ONION SOUP BREAD

1 (12-inch) Dutch oven, 24 hot coals, cooking temperature 350 degrees

MAKES 12 SERVINGS

Cooking spray

Oil

2 cups plus 1 tablespoon buttermilk
(see tip on page 116)

3 tablespoons butter, softened

3 tablespoons molasses

1 envelope onion soup mix

3 ¾ cups flour

¾ cup cornmeal

3 teaspoons active dry yeast

In a large mixing bowl, combine the buttermilk, butter, and molasses until well mixed. Add the soup mix, flour, and cornmeal. Add the yeast and knead on a lightly floured surface until a soft dough forms. Place in a lightly oiled bowl and turn to coat, or leave on floured surface. Cover with a clean cloth and let rise in a warm, draft-free area until double in size. Punch down dough and form into a round loaf. Place in a warmed* Dutch oven that has been prepared with nonstick cooking spray. Cover and let rise until double in size.

Cover with the lid and bake for 40 minutes, or until golden brown, using 10 coals on bottom and 14 on top.

*Tip: To warm the Dutch oven, you can place it in the sun or use about 4 coals underneath the oven for just a few minutes. Remember, you want it warm, not hot.

Tip: You can make your own buttermilk by combining 1 ¾ cups milk with ¼ cup lemon juice.

RUSSIAN BLACK BREAD

1 (12-inch) Dutch oven, 24 hot coals, cooking temperature 350 degrees

MAKES 16 SERVINGS

Cooking spray

Oil

2 ½ cups flour

1 cup rye flour

1 teaspoon salt

2 tablespoons brown sugar

3 tablespoons unsweetened cocoa powder

1 tablespoon caraway seeds

¼ teaspoon fennel seeds

2 teaspoons active dry yeast

4 teaspoons Postum*

2 tablespoons vinegar

2 tablespoons butter, softened

2 tablespoons dark corn syrup

1 ½ cups hot water

In a large mixing bowl, combine flour, rye flour, salt, brown sugar, cocoa powder, caraway seeds, fennel seeds, yeast, and Postum. Add the vinegar, butter, corn syrup, and hot water, and knead on a lightly floured surface until a soft dough forms. Place in a lightly oiled bowl and turn to coat. Cover with a clean cloth and let rise in a warm, draft-free area for 30 minutes, or until double in size. Punch down dough and knead on a lightly floured surface until it becomes smooth and holds its shape, about 10 minutes. Note: the longer you knead the dough, the tougher your bread will be. Form into a round loaf and place in Dutch oven that has been prepared with nonstick cooking spray. Cover and let rise in a warm, draft-free area until double in size.

Cover with the lid and bake for 30–40 minutes, or until the crust is a nice dark brown, using 10 coals underneath the oven and 14 on top.

*1 teaspoon instant coffee granules may be substituted.

JALAPEÑO CHEESE BREAD

1 (12-inch) Dutch oven, 24 hot coals plus extra if needed, cooking temperature 350 degrees

MAKES 16 SERVINGS

3 tablespoons butter, softened, divided

3 eggs, separated into yolks and whites

3 tablespoons sugar

2 cups milk

²/₃ cup cornmeal

²/₃ cup flour

1 teaspoon salt plus 1 pinch salt, divided

2 teaspoons baking powder

¹/₃ cup shredded jalapeño pepper jack cheese, plus extra for sprinkling over top

1 jalapeño, thinly sliced, optional

Preheat Dutch oven using 10 coals underneath the oven. Place 1 tablespoon butter in oven to melt.

In a large mixing bowl, combine remaining butter, egg yolks, and sugar; mix well. Add milk, cornmeal, flour, 1 teaspoon salt, and baking powder. Mix until well combined. Carefully fold in the jalapeño, if using.

In a separate bowl, whip together the egg whites and the pinch of salt until soft peaks form. Fold gently into cornmeal mixture along with the cheese until combined.

Transfer mixture to preheated Dutch oven, cover with the lid, and bake for 20–25 minutes, using 10 coals underneath the oven and 14 on top. Replace coals as needed. Sprinkle more cheese over top during last 5 minutes of baking and let melt.

Tip: To tell if bread is cooked through, thump the bottom of the loaf and listen for a hollow sound.

SOURDOUGH STARTER

MAKES 3 CUPS

2 cups flour

2 cups warm water

1 envelope active dry yeast

Combine flour, warm water, and yeast in a large glass bowl or jar (not metal) and mix together until well blended. Cover loosely with a clean cloth or lid (do not tighten or jar may explode) and leave in a warm place (80–85 degrees) for 48 hours to ferment.

When ready to use, give starter a good stir. Remove amount required by the recipe and replenish starter with equal amounts of flour and water. For example, if 2 cups of starter were removed, replace with 1 cup flour and 1 cup warm water; mix well. Let stand in a warm place for a few hours until it bubbles. Cover loosely and refrigerate. Use and replenish every few weeks.

Note: When measuring flour, spoon into measuring cup and level off. Do not scoop with the cup.

SOURDOUGH BREAD

1 (14-inch) Dutch oven, 26 hot coals, cooking temperature 375 degrees

MAKES 2 LOAVES

Cooking spray

Oil

3 cups hot water (between 80 and
   100 degrees)

2 tablespoons sugar

2 tablespoons active dry yeast

1 tablespoon salt

2 cups Sourdough Starter (facing page)

9 cups flour, divided

In a large mixing bowl, combine water, sugar, and yeast; set aside for 5 minutes. Stir in salt and Sourdough Starter. Add 4 cups flour and stir until dough is smooth. Gradually add enough of the remaining flour to make the dough workable and not sticky. Knead on a lightly floured surface until smooth and elastic. Place in a lightly oiled bowl and turn to coat. Cover with a clean cloth and let rise in a warm, draft-free area for 60 minutes, or until double in size. Punch down dough, remove from bowl, and divide and shape dough into 2 oblong loaves. Place in a warmed* Dutch oven that has been prepared with nonstick cooking spray. Cover and let rise until double in size.

Cover with the lid and bake for 30-40 minutes, using 10 coals underneath the oven and 16 on top. You can tell the bread is done if it sounds hollow when you tap the bottom of the loaf.

*Tip: To warm the Dutch oven, you can place it in the sun or use about 4 coals underneath the oven for just a few minutes. Remember, you want it warm, not hot.

PUMPERNICKEL ROLLS

1 (10-inch) Dutch oven, 20 hot coals, cooking temperature 350 degrees

MAKES 12 ROLLS

Cooking spray

Oil

1 ¼ cups warm water

1 tablespoon sugar

4 ½ teaspoons active dry yeast

1 cup rye flour

1 cup wheat flour

¼ cup molasses

2 tablespoons cocoa powder

1 tablespoon caraway seeds

1 ¼ teaspoons salt

1 ½ cups plus 2 tablespoons flour, divided

In a large mixing bowl, combine water, sugar, and yeast; set aside for 5 minutes. Add rye and wheat flours, molasses, cocoa powder, caraway seeds, and salt; mix well. Stir in 1 cup flour then place on a lightly floured surface. Knead for 5 minutes, gradually adding more flour only if necessary, until dough is smooth and elastic. Place in a lightly oiled bowl and turn to coat. Cover with a clean cloth and let rise in a warm, draft-free area for 60 minutes, or until double in size. Punch down dough, divide into 12 even-size pieces, and roll into balls. Place dough balls in a warmed* Dutch oven that has been prepared with nonstick cooking spray. Cover and let rise 30 minutes, or until double in size.

Cover with the lid and bake for 30 minutes, or until tops are golden brown, using 8 coals underneath the oven and 12 on top.

*Tip: To warm the Dutch oven, you can place it in the sun or use about 4 coals underneath the oven for just a few minutes. Remember, you want it warm, not hot.

ONE-BOWL DINNER ROLLS

1 (12-inch) Dutch oven, 26 hot coals, cooking temperature 375 degrees

MAKES 16 ROLLS

Cooking spray

2 ¾ to 3 ¼ cups flour, divided

¾ cup sugar

½ teaspoon salt

2 tablespoons active dry yeast

5 ⅓ tablespoons butter, softened

⅔ cup hot water

1 egg, at room temperature, beaten

1 teaspoon garlic powder

1 teaspoon onion powder

2 teaspoons dried rosemary

In a large mixing bowl, mix together ¾ cup flour, sugar, salt, and yeast. Add butter and water. Stir until well combined and a thick batter forms. Stir in egg, ½ cup flour, garlic powder, onion powder, and rosemary. Knead in bowl, gradually adding enough of the remaining flour until a soft dough forms. Knead for 2 minutes, or until smooth. Cover with a clean cloth and let rise in a warm, draft-free area until double in size. Punch down dough, divide into 16 even-size pieces, and roll into balls. Place dough balls in a warmed* Dutch oven that has been prepared with nonstick cooking spray. Cover and let rise until double in size.

Cover with the lid and bake for 10-15 minutes, or until golden brown, using 10 coals underneath the oven and 16 on top.

*Tip: To warm the Dutch oven, you can place it in the sun or use about 4 coals underneath the oven for just a few minutes. Remember, you want it warm, not hot.

GOLDEN HONEY SOURDOUGH ROLLS

1 (12-inch) Dutch oven, 24 hot coals, cooking temperature 350 degrees

MAKES 16 ROLLS

Cooking spray

Oil

2 cups scalded milk

2 tablespoons butter

¼ cup honey

1 tablespoon active dry yeast

4 cups Sourdough Starter (page 38)

2 cups wheat flour

¼ cup wheat germ, optional

2 teaspoons baking soda

2 tablespoons salt

2 tablespoons sugar

2 cups flour

In a small mixing bowl, combine milk, butter, and honey; stir until well mixed. Set aside to cool until lukewarm. Add yeast and stir until dissolved.

In a large mixing bowl, combine Sourdough Starter, wheat flour, and wheat germ, if using.

In a small bowl, combine baking soda, salt, and sugar; add to sourdough mixture and gently combine. Add yeast mixture and mix well. Cover with a clean cloth and let sit 30 minutes. Stir down dough and gradually add remaining flour until too stiff to stir with a spoon (amount of flour may vary). Place on a lightly floured surface and knead until smooth and elastic then place in a lightly oiled bowl and turn to coat. Cover and let rise in a warm, draft-free area until double in size. Punch down dough, divide into 16 even-size pieces, and roll into balls. Place in a warmed* Dutch oven that has been prepared with nonstick cooking spray, cover, and let rise until double in size.

Cover with the lid and bake for 20 minutes, or until golden brown, using 10 coals underneath the oven and 14 on top. Remove from Dutch oven and cool on a wire rack.

*Tip: To warm the Dutch oven, you can place it in the sun or use about 4 coals underneath the oven for just a few minutes. Remember, you want it warm, not hot.

PARMESAN-HERB TWISTS

1 (14-inch) Dutch oven, 34 hot coals, cooking temperature 375 degrees

MAKES 16 ROLLS

Cooking spray

Oil

1 cup warm milk

1 cup warm water

4 ½ teaspoons active dry yeast

6 tablespoons butter, melted

3 eggs, well beaten

1 teaspoon salt

½ cup sugar

1 teaspoon garlic powder

1 teaspoon onion powder

1 teaspoon crushed dried rosemary

3 tablespoons freshly grated Parmesan cheese, plus extra for topping

6 ½ cups flour, divided

In a large mixing bowl, stir together the milk, water, and yeast. Add butter, eggs, salt, sugar, garlic powder, onion powder, rosemary, and Parmesan cheese. Add 3 cups flour and mix well to combine. Gradually add remaining flour and knead until a soft dough forms. Place in a lightly oiled bowl and turn to coat. Cover with a towel and let rise in a warm, draft-free area until double in size.

Punch down dough, divide into 16 even-size pieces, and roll into balls. Divide each ball in half and roll the halves into 6-inch ropes. Twist 2 ropes together, pinching the ends to seal, and place in Dutch oven that has been prepared with nonstick cooking spray. Repeat with remaining ropes. Cover and let rise until double in size.

Cover with the lid and bake for 20-30 minutes, or until golden brown, using 12 coals underneath the oven and 22 on top. Remove from Dutch oven and sprinkle with more cheese. Cool on a wire rack.

MAIN
DISHES

THE KING'S CHICKEN

1 (12-inch) Dutch oven, 34 hot coals, cooking temperature 350 degrees

MAKES 8 TO 10 SERVINGS

Cooking spray

1 tablespoon butter

½ cup shredded Monterey Jack cheese

¼ cup chopped fresh chives

¼ cup chopped fresh parsley

1½ teaspoons salt

1 teaspoon orange zest, divided

⅛ teaspoon pepper

¼ cup chopped fresh spinach

2 eggs

½ cup orange juice

4 tablespoons flour

1 cup breadcrumbs

6 boneless, skinless chicken breasts, flattened to ¼ inch thick

1 recipe Creamy White Mushroom Sauce (page 96)

In a medium mixing bowl, combine butter, cheese, chives, parsley, salt, ½ teaspoon orange zest, pepper, and spinach; form into 6 finger-size pieces and chill until firm.

In a separate bowl, mix together the eggs, orange juice, and flour until well combined. Pour batter into Dutch oven and heat, using 10 coals underneath the oven, stirring constantly until slightly thickened. Remove from heat and set aside to cool. When the Dutch oven is cool enough to handle, pour batter into a separate bowl and wipe Dutch oven out with a clean lint-free cloth.

In a small bowl, thoroughly mix breadcrumbs and remaining orange zest together; set aside.

Roll 1 of the chilled filling pieces in each flattened chicken breast and secure with a toothpick, if necessary. Dip in batter and roll in breadcrumb mixture to coat. Place in Dutch oven that has been prepared with nonstick cooking spray. Cover with the lid and bake for 45 minutes, using 10 coals underneath the oven and 14 on top. Serve with Creamy White Mushroom Sauce over top.

TERIYAKI-BARBECUE CHICKEN

1 (14-inch) Dutch oven, 28 hot coals, cooking temperature 350 degrees

MAKES 6 TO 8 SERVINGS

1 (18-ounce) bottle teriyaki sauce

1 (18-ounce) bottle barbecue sauce

6 to 8 boneless, skinless chicken breasts

1 (12-ounce) can lemon-lime soda

Pour the teriyaki and barbecue sauces into the Dutch oven, stir to combine, and add the chicken. Pour soda evenly over top. Cover with the lid and bake for 30 minutes, or until done, using 12 coals underneath the oven and 16 on top.

CATALINA CHICKEN

1 (12-inch) Dutch oven, 24 hot coals plus extra if needed, cooking temperature 350 degrees

MAKES 8 TO 10 SERVINGS

3 to 4 pounds chicken leg and thigh pieces, skin removed*

1 (24-ounce) bottle Catalina salad dressing

Layer chicken in Dutch oven and pour dressing evenly over top. Cover with the lid and bake for 60 minutes, or until chicken starts to fall off the bones, using 10 coals underneath the oven and 14 on top. Replace coals as needed.

*Tip: Boneless, skinless chicken breasts may be substituted, in which case the cooking time may be shorter.

CHICKEN ROLL-UPS

1 (12-inch) Dutch oven, 24 hot coals, cooking temperature 350 degrees

MAKES 4 TO 6 SERVINGS

1 recipe Creamy White Mushroom Sauce (page 96)

4 to 6 thin slices ham

4 to 6 thin slices Asiago cheese

4 to 6 boneless, skinless chicken breasts, flattened to ¼ inch thick

4 to 6 slices peppered bacon, optional

Salt and pepper, to taste

Prepare the Creamy White Mushroom Sauce and then transfer to the 12-inch oven you will be using for cooking the chicken rolls.

Place 1 slice ham and 1 slice cheese on top of each chicken breast. Starting from the short side, roll up the chicken breast and fillings, tuck in ends, and wrap with 1 slice bacon, if using; secure with toothpicks.

Place chicken rolls in Dutch oven with the mushroom sauce, cover with the lid and bake for 30–40 minutes, or until done, using 10 coals underneath the oven and 14 on top. Season with salt and pepper before serving.

Variation: For bacon lovers, use 2 slices bacon per chicken breast.

APRICOT AND RASPBERRY-GLAZED HENS

1 deep (14-inch) Dutch oven with rack, 45 hot coals plus extra if needed, cooking temperature 450 degrees. This recipe requires a 24-hour prep time.

MAKES 3 TO 5 SERVINGS

3 to 5 Cornish hens

1 (11.5-ounce) can apricot nectar

1 cup raspberry vinaigrette

1 cup apricot jam

1 tablespoon all-purpose poultry seasoning

Salt and pepper, to taste

3 to 10 fresh rosemary sprigs

Rinse hens thoroughly and pat dry with paper towels. Inject apricot nectar into breasts of hens 24 hours before cooking and refrigerate.

In a small bowl, mix the vinaigrette and jam together; set aside.

Preheat Dutch oven to 450 degrees, using 22 coals underneath the oven and 23 on top. Rub the outside of the hens with seasoning and salt and pepper. Place 1 or 2 sprigs of rosemary inside the cavity of each hen. Place hens on a rack in Dutch oven, breast side up, cover with the lid, and bake for 45–60 minutes. Replace coals as needed.

Remove a few coals* to reduce heat as hens begin to brown to prevent burning. Brush hens with half of the jam mixture about 20 minutes before they are finished cooking. When fully cooked,** remove hens to a serving dish and remove and discard the rosemary. Brush remaining jam mixture evenly over each hen just before serving.

*When you remove 1 coal, the heat will be reduced by approximately 20 degrees.

**If the little drumsticks can be easily pulled away from the body of the bird, it is fully cooked.

EASY CHICKEN AND RICE

1 (14-inch) Dutch oven, 28 hot coals plus extra if needed, cooking temperature 350 degrees

MAKES 6 TO 8 SERVINGS

2 cups uncooked white rice

2 (10.5-ounce) cans condensed cream of chicken, mushroom, or celery soup

4 cups water

6 boneless, skinless chicken breasts

1 envelope dry onion soup mix

Shredded cheddar cheese, to taste

Stir together the rice, cream soup, and water in the Dutch oven until well blended. Place chicken breasts over rice mixture and sprinkle evenly with dry soup mix. Cover with the lid and bake for 60 minutes, or until the rice is cooked and the chicken is done (juices run clear), using 10 coals underneath the oven and 18 on top. Replace coals as needed. Sprinkle cheese over top and let melt before serving.

DUTCH OVEN POT ROAST

1 (12-inch) Dutch oven, 24 hot coals plus extra if needed, cooking temperature 350 degrees

MAKES 6 TO 8 SERVINGS

1 envelope dry onion soup mix

1 (3- to 4-pound) beef roast

1 ½ cups water, plus extra as needed, divided

2 beef bouillon cubes

½ pound baby carrots

8 to 10 medium red or new potatoes

2 tablespoons flour

Preheat Dutch oven using all 24 coals underneath the oven.

Rub dry soup mix over the entire roast, place in preheated oven, and sear until browned on all sides. Add 1 cup water and the bouillon. Cover with the lid and bake for 30 minutes, using 10 coals underneath the oven and 14 on top. Replace coals as needed to maintain cooking temperature.

Check and add water as needed, keeping the bottom of the oven covered with liquid. Add carrots and potatoes, cover, and continue to bake for 30 more minutes, or until vegetables are tender and roast is cooked to an internal temperature of 160 degrees. Remove roast from oven to a serving platter and let rest for a few minutes. Remove vegetables to a serving bowl and cover to keep warm.

To make a gravy, bring drippings in Dutch oven to a boil; add flour and remaining ½ cup water, stirring constantly until smooth and starting to thicken. Spoon gravy over roast and vegetables to serve.

CHICKEN PILLOWS

1 (12-inch) Dutch oven, 44 hot coals, cooking temperature 350 degrees

MAKES 8 SERVINGS

Cooking spray, optional

2 boneless, skinless chicken breasts, cut into 1-inch pieces

2 bunches green onions, white part only, thinly sliced

1 (8-ounce) package cream cheese, softened

2 (8-ounce) cans refrigerated crescent roll dough

Brown and cook chicken pieces thoroughly in Dutch oven, using 20 coals underneath the oven. Remove to a plate and set aside to cool.

In a medium mixing bowl, stir onions into cream cheese until well mixed. Add cooled chicken and stir to combine.

Separate crescent dough into individual triangles. Using a tablespoon, place a scoop of chicken mixture on each piece of dough and roll up, starting with the wide end. There should be enough mixture to fill 16 rolls. Place filled rolls in Dutch oven.* Cover with the lid and bake for 12–15 minutes, or until golden brown, using 10 coals underneath the oven and 14 on top. Remove from oven and serve while still hot.

Variation: If you like gravy, try serving these with chicken or turkey gravy drizzled over top.

*Tip: Depending on your Dutch oven, you may want to use a nonstick cooking spray on the bottom to prevent the rolls from sticking. However, if your oven is well-seasoned from use, they should slide out of the oven nicely with the help of a rubber spatula.

STUFFED FLANK STEAK

1 (14-inch) Dutch oven, 34–38 hot coals plus extra if needed, cooking temperature 350 degrees

MAKES 8 SERVINGS

1 (1- to 2-pound) flank steak, flattened to ¼ inch thick

Salt and pepper, to taste

¼ cup toasted pine nuts

⅓ cup chopped fresh mint

½ cup chopped fresh parsley

5 cloves garlic, peeled and crushed

¼ cup freshly grated Parmesan cheese

1 lemon, juiced

2 tablespoons olive oil, divided

1 to 2 cups Fresh Tomato Sauce (page 93)

Sprinkle both sides of steak with salt and pepper. Place in refrigerator or cooler until ready to use.

In a small bowl, combine nuts, mint, parsley, garlic, cheese, lemon juice, and 1 tablespoon oil; stir together. Remove steak from refrigerator and spread mixture evenly over one side. Roll the steak up across the grain like a jelly roll and tie with kitchen twine to secure at each end and in the middle. Season with more salt and pepper.

In a warm Dutch oven using 18 to 20 coals underneath the oven, add remaining oil and sear the stuffed steak until browned on all sides. Pour Fresh Tomato Sauce over top, bring to a boil, and remove some of the coals, leaving 10 to 12 underneath the oven. Cover with the lid and place 16 to 18 fresh coals on top. Bring to a simmer and cook for 60 minutes, turning steak a few times during cooking. Replace coals as needed.

Remove steak from oven to a serving platter and let rest for 10-15 minutes. Remove and discard the twine and slice steak into ½-inch-thick pieces. Serve with warm sauce drizzled over top.

SLOPPY JOES

1 (12-inch) Dutch oven, 30 hot coals, cooking temperature 350 degrees

MAKES 4 TO 6 SERVINGS

1 pound ground beef

1 (10.75-ounce) can chicken gumbo soup

1/2 cup ketchup

1/8 cup mustard

1/2 medium onion, chopped

1 (8-ounce) can tomato sauce

2 tablespoons Worcestershire sauce

4 to 6 hamburger buns

In Dutch oven, brown the ground beef until cooked through, using 30 coals underneath the oven; drain the grease. Add the soup, ketchup, mustard, onion, tomato sauce, and Worcestershire sauce. Mix to combine. Remove enough coals from underneath the oven to achieve a simmer. Cover with the lid and simmer for 30 minutes, stirring occasionally to prevent burning. Serve in buns.

STUFFED PORK ROAST

1 (14-inch) Dutch oven, 26 hot coals plus extra as needed, cooking temperature 350 degrees

MAKES 8 SERVINGS

1 (2- to 3-pound) boneless pork roast

Salt and pepper, to taste

2 tablespoons toasted pine nuts

1/2 cup chopped fresh mint

1/2 cup chopped fresh parsley

6 to 8 cloves garlic, peeled and crushed

1/2 cup freshly grated Parmesan cheese

1 lemon, juiced

2 tablespoons olive oil, divided

1 recipe Fresh Tomato Sauce (page 93)

Place meat on a cutting board and slice lengthwise down the center of the roast, cutting only two-thirds of the way through. Press each side apart and make another lengthwise cut down the center of each side, cutting only two-thirds through. Pound roast until it lays flat. Season with salt and pepper.

In a small bowl, combine nuts, mint, parsley, garlic, cheese, lemon juice, and 1 tablespoon oil. Stir together until combined and spread evenly over roast. Roll up the roast tightly, like a jelly roll, and tie together with kitchen twine to secure at each end and in the middle. Season with more salt and pepper.

Heat Dutch oven using 10 coals underneath the oven and 16 on top. Add remaining oil and brown roast on all sides. Add tomato sauce, cover, and bring to a boil. Reduce heat to a simmer by removing several coals from the top.

Simmer gently for 60 minutes, or until internal temperature reaches 145 degrees, turning roast a few times during cooking. Replace coals as needed.

Remove roast from Dutch oven to a serving plate and let rest for 15 minutes. Remove and discard twine and slice roast into 1/2-inch-thick pieces. Serve with warm sauce drizzled over top.

MEAT AND CHEESE-STUFFED MANICOTTI

1 (10-inch) Dutch oven and 1 (12-inch) Dutch oven, 48 hot coals plus extra as needed, cooking temperature 350 degrees

MAKES 4 TO 6 SERVINGS

1 (1.37-ounce) packet spaghetti sauce mix

1 pound ground beef

¼ pound shredded Asiago or other
   sharp cheese

1 (8-ounce) can tomato sauce

1 (8-ounce) package uncooked
   manicotti shells

½ pound shredded Monterey Jack cheese

Using 10 coals underneath the 10-inch Dutch oven, make the spaghetti sauce according to package directions and gently simmer.

Brown the ground beef in the 12-inch Dutch oven until cooked through, using 12 to 14 coals underneath the oven; drain grease. Place the cooked beef in a bowl to cool. Once cooled, add the Asiago cheese to beef and stir in the tomato sauce until combined. Gently stuff the manicotti shells with the meat mixture.

Pour enough spaghetti sauce into the bottom of the 12-inch Dutch oven just to cover. Arrange stuffed manicotti over sauce. Spoon any leftover beef mixture over top followed by remaining spaghetti sauce; sprinkle evenly with Monterey Jack cheese. Cover with the lid and bake for 40-45 minutes, or until manicotti shells are soft, using 10 coals underneath the oven and 14 on top. Replace coals as needed.

FAVORITE DUTCH OVEN LASAGNA

1 (14-inch) Dutch oven, 28 hot coals, cooking temperature 350 degrees

MAKES 16 SERVINGS

1 (16-ounce) package lasagna noodles

1 ½ pounds ground beef, cooked
and drained

1 large onion, chopped

3 cloves garlic, peeled and minced

2 (24-ounce) jars spaghetti sauce
of choice

1 (32-ounce) carton small-curd
cottage cheese

2 eggs, beaten

1 (8-ounce) package cream
cheese, softened

2 pounds shredded mozzarella cheese

Cook lasagna noodles according to package directions; drain and set aside.

In a large mixing bowl, mix together the beef, onion, and garlic. Add the spaghetti sauce and stir to combine. In a separate bowl, combine the cottage cheese, eggs, and cream cheese.

Layer one-third of the meat mixture, one-third noodles, and one-third cottage cheese mixture in the bottom of the Dutch oven. Repeat layers and sprinkle mozzarella cheese evenly over top. Cover with the lid and bake for 45 minutes, or until cheese melts and the sauce is bubbly, using 10 coals underneath the oven and 18 on top.

HOMEMADE DUTCH OVEN PIZZA

1 (12-inch) Dutch oven, 28 hot coals, cooking temperature 425 degrees

MAKES 8 SERVINGS

Cooking spray

¾ cup warm water

2 tablespoons vegetable oil

2 cups flour

½ teaspoon sugar

½ teaspoon salt

2 teaspoons active dry yeast

Tomato or pizza sauce of choice

Favorite pizza toppings

2 cups shredded mozzarella cheese

In a large mixing bowl, mix together the water, oil, flour, sugar, salt, and yeast until well combined. Cover with a clean cloth and let rise in a warm, draft-free area for 20–30 minutes, or until double in size.

Place dough in Dutch oven that has been prepared with nonstick cooking spray. Flatten gently, pressing from the center of the oven to the edges and slightly up the sides to form a crust. Spread desired amount of tomato sauce over dough and layer with your favorite toppings and cheese. Cover with the lid and bake for 20–25 minutes, or until cheese is melted and bubbly and crust is cooked on the bottom, using 10 coals underneath the oven and 18 on top. When done, carefully remove pizza from oven by tilting gently while a helper slides spatulas under the crust and guides it onto a rack or large plate.

Tip: To make removing the pizza from the Dutch oven a lot easier, fit and layer the bottom and sides of the oven with a large round piece of parchment paper before adding the dough. This way you can lift the cooked pizza out of the oven by using the parchment paper as handles.

Variation: Need a bigger pizza? Double ingredients and bake in a 14-inch Dutch oven at 425 degrees, using 12 coals underneath the oven and 20 on top.

SWEET-AND-SOUR DUTCH OVEN

1 (14-inch) Dutch oven, 22-30 hot coals plus extra as needed, cooking temperature 375-400 degrees

MAKES 12 SERVINGS

4 pounds beef, pork, or chicken, cut into
   1-inch chunks

4 pounds carrots, peeled and sliced

1 tablespoon olive oil

1 cup chopped onion

4 pounds sliced fresh mushrooms

Water

1 (10-ounce) bottle soy sauce

1 (24-ounce) bottle ketchup

1 1/2 cups sugar

1/4 cup vinegar

2 (20-ounce) cans pineapple chunks,
   drained, juice reserved

2 green bell peppers, diced

Cornstarch

Hot cooked rice, for serving

Sliced green onions, for garnish, optional

Using 20 coals underneath the Dutch oven, stir-fry the meat and carrots in oil until meat is cooked through. Add the onion and mushrooms and cook until mushrooms are tender. Add enough water to just cover the bottom of the oven. Add soy sauce, ketchup, sugar, vinegar, and reserved pineapple juice; stir until combined. Bring to a boil and cook, uncovered, for 35-40 minutes, or until the color of the sauce is a burnt orange, using 22 to 30 coals underneath the oven. Replace coals as needed.

Stir in the bell peppers and add enough cornstarch to the sauce until it is thickened as desired. Remove from heat and stir in pineapple. Serve over hot rice and garnish with onions, if desired.

CHILE VERDE

1 (12-inch) Dutch oven, 24 hot coals plus extra as needed, cooking temperature 350 degrees

MAKES 8 SERVINGS

6 pork chops, cut into 1-inch pieces

½ pound ground beef

2 tablespoons olive oil

1 onion, chopped

1 clove garlic, peeled and chopped

3 (4-ounce) cans chopped green chiles

2 (14.5-ounce) cans stewed tomatoes, drained

1 jalapeño, seeds removed and chopped

½ teaspoon salt

⅛ teaspoon freshly ground black pepper

16 medium flour tortillas, warmed

3 cups shredded cheddar cheese

In Dutch oven, brown the pork and beef in oil until meat is cooked through, using 20 coals underneath the oven; drain the grease. Add the onion, garlic, green chiles, tomatoes, jalapeño, salt, and pepper. Cover with the lid and bake for 45–60 minutes, or until meat is tender, using 10 coals underneath the oven and 14 on top, stirring occasionally. Replace coals as needed. Serve over warmed tortillas topped with cheese.

STUFFED PORK CHOPS IN MUSHROOM GRAVY

1 (12-inch) Dutch oven, 44 hot coals plus extra as needed, cooking temperature 350 degrees

MAKES 4 SERVINGS

1 (8-ounce) package sliced fresh
   mushrooms, divided

3 cups breadcrumbs

3 to 4 green onions, thinly sliced

1/3 red bell pepper, diced

2 cloves garlic, minced

1 stalk celery, diced

1/2 teaspoon salt

1 3/4 teaspoons ground sage

1/2 cup shelled and roasted
   sunflower seeds

6 tablespoons butter, melted

1/2 cup evaporated milk

4 center-cut pork loin chops, about
   1 inch thick

1/2 cup pork rub, divided

1 packet onion gravy mix

In a large mixing bowl, add half the mushrooms, the breadcrumbs, green onions, bell pepper, garlic, celery, salt, sage, sunflower seeds, butter, and milk. Mix together until the breadcrumbs are completely moistened and then place in refrigerator or cooler.

Using a sharp knife, cut a horizontal slit about two-thirds of the way through each pork chop to make a pocket for the stuffing. Use 1/4 cup of the pork rub to season and rub on both sides of each chop. Place chops in heated Dutch oven, using 20 coals underneath the oven, and sear on both sides. Remove chops from oven to a plate and refrigerate until ready to stuff.

Make gravy according to package directions; stir in remaining pork rub and mushrooms. Remove pork chops and filling from the refrigerator. Divide the filling evenly between the chops and stuff; secure with toothpicks if necessary. Place chops back in Dutch oven with the gravy. Cover with the lid and bake for 30-40 minutes, or until the internal temperature reaches 165 degrees, using 10 coals underneath the oven and 14 on top. Replace coals as needed. Serve with mushroom gravy.

STUFFED PORK TENDERLOINS IN FRESH TOMATO SAUCE

1 (12-inch) Dutch oven, 48 hot coals plus extra as needed, cooking temperature 350 degrees

MAKES 8 SERVINGS

⅔ (8-ounce) can whole water chestnuts, drained and chopped

6 to 8 ounces frozen chopped spinach, partially thawed

1 (8-ounce) package cream cheese, softened

1 to 2 green onions, green stalks only, chopped

1 (1.4-ounce) packet Knorr Vegetable Recipe Mix

2 (1-pound) pork tenderloins

Vegetable oil, for browning

1 recipe Fresh Tomato Sauce (page 93)

In a medium mixing bowl, combine water chestnuts, spinach, cream cheese, green onions, and Knorr mix; set aside.

With a sharp knife, make a lengthwise cut down the center of each tenderloin, cutting two-thirds of the way through. Press sides apart and make another lengthwise cut down the middle of each side, cutting only two-thirds of the way through.

Brown the tenderloins on all sides in a small amount of oil in Dutch oven, using 20 to 24 coals underneath the oven. Remove tenderloins and set aside to cool. Once cooled, divide the spinach mixture in half and spread evenly over each tenderloin. Roll up the tenderloins tightly, like a jelly roll, and tie each one with kitchen twine to secure at each end and in the middle. Place in Dutch oven and pour tomato sauce over top. Cover with the lid and bake for 35–40 minutes, or until the internal temperature reaches 160 degrees, using 10 coals underneath the oven and 14 on top. Replace coals as needed. Serve with warm sauce drizzled over top.

SAUSAGE-SPINACH WREATH

1 (12-inch) Camp Chef Ultimate Dutch Oven, 35 hot coals, cooking temperature 400 degrees

MAKES 12 TO 16 SERVINGS

½ pound ground pork, browned and drained

½ pound pork sausage, browned and drained

1 (8-ounce) package cream cheese, softened

1 (8-ounce) can water chestnuts, drained and chopped

1 (1.4-ounce) packet Knorr Vegetable Recipe Mix

6 ounces chopped frozen spinach, thawed

1 to 2 green onions, green stalks only, chopped

2 (10 x 15-inch) sheets frozen puff pastry, thawed

In a large bowl, mix together all of the ingredients except puff pastry; cover and set aside. Cut off corners of both sheets of pastry, making them into 10-inch circles. Cut each circle into 8 even wedges, for a total of 16.

Cover Dutch oven rack with parchment paper and arrange 7 pastry wedges in a circle with wide edges touching or slightly overlapping and points facing out. Arrange 7 more wedges in the center of the circle, matching wide ends with wedges already in place, slightly overlapping, points facing center (points will overlap). Lightly press the side edges together to seal. Discard unused pastry.

Spoon meat mixture evenly over the wide overlapped edges of the pastry to form a circle. Beginning with last pastry wedge that was placed in the center, lift point and lay straight across meat mixture, tucking the point underneath the pastry. Lift the point from opposite outside wedge diagonally across point of previous wedge and lay across meat mixture, tucking point underneath pastry. Continue alternating points until a wreath is formed; some filling will show.

Cut 3 or 4 slits in the center of the parchment paper so that it will slide easily over the center convection cone and place rack in a warmed* Dutch oven. Cover with the lid and bake for 40-50 minutes, or until golden brown, using 15 coals underneath the oven and 20 on top.

*Tip: To warm the Dutch oven, you can place it in the sun or use about 4 coals underneath the oven for just a few minutes. Remember, you want it warm, not hot.

SIDE DISHES

HONEY-GLAZED CARROTS

1 (10-inch) Dutch oven, 18 hot coals, cooking temperature 325 degrees

MAKES 6 SERVINGS

¼ cup butter

1 pound peeled and cut baby carrots

½ cup honey

2 tablespoons brown sugar

Place butter in a warmed* Dutch oven and melt. Add carrots to melted butter, pour honey over top, and sprinkle evenly with brown sugar; stir to coat. Cover with the lid and bake for 30 minutes, or until carrots are fork tender, using 8 coals underneath the oven and 10 on top.

*Tip: To warm the Dutch oven, you can place it in the sun or use about 4 coals underneath the oven for just a few minutes. Remember, you want it warm, not hot.

POTATOES, ONION, AND BACON

1 (12-inch) Dutch oven, 44–48 hot coals plus extra if needed, cooking temperature 350 degrees

MAKES 8 SERVINGS

½ to 1 pound bacon, cut into 1-inch pieces

1 medium onion, sliced

6 to 8 red potatoes, sliced

Salt and pepper, to taste

Cook the bacon in Dutch oven, using 20 to 24 coals underneath the oven. When the bacon is almost cooked, add the onion and continue to cook until the bacon is to your liking. Add the potatoes, salt and pepper, and stir to combine.

Remove the coals you used to cook the bacon. Cover with the lid and bake for 90 minutes, or until potatoes are tender, but not overcooked, using 10 new coals underneath the oven and 14 new coals on top, stirring every 10–15 minutes. Replace coals as needed.

CHEESY POTATOES

2 (12-inch) Dutch ovens, 48-53 hot coals, cooking temperature 350 degrees

MAKES 12 SERVINGS

6 large potatoes*

¼ cup butter, melted

2 cups sour cream

1 (10.5-ounce) can condensed cream of chicken soup

¼ cup chopped onion

4 cups shredded cheddar cheese, divided

In one of the Dutch ovens, add the potatoes and enough water to completely cover. Cover with the lid and boil the potatoes until fork-tender, using 24 coals underneath the oven and 5 on top. Remove potatoes from oven and set aside to cool. When potatoes have cooled enough to handle, grate them into a large bowl.

Empty the potato water from oven and add the butter, sour cream, soup, and onion. Stir to combine and bring to a simmer for 5 minutes, using the same 24 coals you cooked the potatoes with. Replace coals as needed.

In the second Dutch oven, layer one-third each of the sauce, potatoes, and cheese in that order. Repeat layers until all ingredients are used, finishing with a layer of cheese. Cover with the lid and bake for 20 minutes, or until bubbly and cheese has melted, using 10 coals underneath the oven and 14 on top.

*Tip: If you are in a hurry, you can skip the first step of boiling and grating the potatoes by substituting 1 (2-pound) bag frozen Southern-style hash brown potatoes that have been thawed.

CORN ON THE COB

1 (12-inch) Dutch oven with a rack, 30 hot coals, cooking temperature 350 degrees

MAKES 6 SERVINGS

6 cobs fresh sweet corn, still in husks   ½ cup water

Trim ends of corn and husks. Remove outer husk layer, leaving 2 inner layers. Pull inner layers back slightly to remove silk. Fold husk back over the corn.

Place rack in Dutch oven, add water, and bring to a boil using 30 coals underneath the oven. Layer corn on the rack, cover with the lid, and let steam for 10–20 minutes, or until corn kernels are tender. Remove from Dutch oven and serve immediately.

DUTCH OVEN POTATOES

1 (12-inch) Dutch oven, 48 hot coals plus extra as needed, cooking temperature 350 degrees

MAKES 12 TO 14 SERVINGS

1 pound bacon, cut into 1-inch pieces

10 medium russet potatoes, peeled and thinly sliced

5 carrots, peeled and thinly sliced, optional

2 medium onions, diced

Salt and pepper, to taste

1 (10.5-ounce) can condensed cream of mushroom soup

1 (24-ounce) container sour cream

1 (8-ounce) package sliced fresh mushrooms

1 pound shredded cheddar cheese

In Dutch oven, brown bacon pieces until crisp, using 10 to 12 coals underneath the oven, stirring frequently to prevent burning. Remove bacon and let drain on a paper towel; set aside.

Drain half the grease from the oven and add the potatoes, carrots, if using, and onions. Stir well and add enough water to cover 1 inch in bottom of oven. Season with salt and pepper. Cover with the lid and bake for 35-40 minutes, or until potatoes and carrots are tender, using 10 coals underneath the oven and 14 on top. Replace coals as needed.

In a small bowl, stir soup and sour cream together until smooth. Add soup mixture, mushrooms, and bacon to the potatoes; stir gently to mix. Cover and bake for 10 minutes more. Sprinkle cheese evenly over top and cover until cheese melts.

FRESH TOMATO SAUCE

1 (12-inch) Dutch oven, 18-20 hot coals plus extra if needed, cooking temperature 350 degrees

MAKES 2 CUPS

2 tablespoons olive oil

4 to 8 cloves garlic, peeled and crushed

1/4 medium onion, finely chopped

1 tomato, cored and chopped

1 (14-ounce) can Italian stewed tomatoes, with liquid

1/4 cup chopped fresh parsley

1 (14-ounce) can chicken broth

1/2 teaspoon dried marjoram

1/2 teaspoon dried rosemary, crushed

1 1/2 tablespoons butter

Salt and pepper, to taste

Heat Dutch oven to 350 degrees using 18 to 20 coals underneath the oven. Add oil, garlic, and onion and sauté until onion is translucent. Add the tomato, stewed tomatoes with liquid, parsley, broth, marjoram, and rosemary; stir to combine. Bring to a boil and then remove enough coals to reduce sauce to a gentle simmer. Cover with the lid and simmer for about 60 minutes, stirring occasionally. Replace coals as needed. Stir in butter and salt and pepper.

This sauce is great served over chicken, pork, or your favorite pasta, or as a pizza sauce, if thickened a bit.

Tip: If you would like a thicker sauce, simmer uncovered, stirring occasionally, until sauce has cooked down to desired consistency.

CREAMY PARMESAN SAUCE

1 (8-inch) Dutch oven, 6 hot coals plus extra if needed, cooking temperature 300 degrees

MAKES 2 CUPS

1 (10.75-ounce) can condensed cream of mushroom soup

1 cup milk

2 tablespoons chopped fresh parsley

$\frac{1}{2}$ cup butter

$\frac{3}{4}$ cup freshly grated Parmesan cheese

Salt and pepper, to taste

Place soup, milk, and parsley in the Dutch oven; mix until smooth. Add butter and bring mixture to a simmer, using 6 coals underneath the oven. Stir frequently until butter melts and sauce is heated through. Add cheese and stir until completely melted and incorporated into sauce. Season with salt and pepper. Replace coals as needed.

Serve over steamed fresh vegetables, such as broccoli, asparagus, or baby red potatoes. Or stir it into your favorite pasta and add some vegetables and chicken for a nice main dish.

CREAMY WHITE MUSHROOM SAUCE

1 (10-inch) Dutch oven, 10 hot coals, cooking temperature 350 degrees

MAKES 2 CUPS

1 (8-ounce) package sliced
   fresh mushrooms

3 tablespoons flour

3 tablespoons butter

½ cup chicken broth

1 cup light cream or whipping cream

¼ cup pimientos

2 teaspoons Dijon mustard

Place mushrooms in large zip-top bag and sprinkle flour over top; seal bag and shake to coat.

Melt butter in Dutch oven, using 10 coals underneath the oven. Add mushrooms and sauté for 5 minutes, or until mushrooms are tender. Add broth and cream and cook until sauce thickens, stirring frequently. Stir in pimientos and mustard.

This is a nice, versatile sauce. Serve over pork chops, use as a base to simmer chicken in, or add some chopped fresh herbs and toss with fettuccini noodles.

TORTILLA SOUP

1 (12-inch) Dutch oven, 29 hot coals, plus extra if needed, cooking temperature 375 degrees

MAKES 15 TO 20 SERVINGS

4 tablespoons olive oil, plus extra if needed

24 (6-inch) corn tortillas, cut into
   1-inch pieces

1 large onion, chopped

3 cloves garlic, peeled and finely chopped

1 red bell pepper, seeded and chopped

4 yellow wax peppers, seeded and chopped

4 boneless, skinless chicken breasts, cut
   into bite-size chunks

3 quarts water

2 tablespoons pasilla chile powder

2 tablespoons New Mexico chile powder

2 tablespoons California chile powder

2 (16-ounce) cans diced or stewed
   tomatoes, with liquid

1 tablespoon salt

1 pound shredded Monterey Jack cheese

4 ripe avocados, cut into bite-size chunks,
   for garnish

Heat the Dutch oven to 375 degrees using 10 to 13 coals underneath the oven. Add enough oil to just cover bottom of oven. Place tortilla pieces, a handful at a time, in hot oil and fry until golden brown. Remove from oil and drain on paper towels; set tortillas aside.

Sauté onion, garlic, bell pepper, and yellow peppers in hot oil until onion is translucent. Add chicken and brown until cooked through. Add water, chile powders, tomatoes, and salt; stir. Cover with the lid and simmer for 15 minutes, using the same 13 coals underneath the oven and 16 on top. Replace coals as needed. Just before serving, add the fried tortilla squares to the soup.

To serve, place some cheese in the bottom of individual soup bowls and ladle the hot soup over the cheese. Garnish with avocado chunks.

CHUNKY CHICKEN SOUP

1 deep (12-inch) Dutch oven, 10 hot coals plus extra if needed, cooking temperature 350 degrees

MAKES 10 TO 12 SERVINGS

1 (24-ounce) bottle ketchup

2 (12-ounce) cans cola

6 boneless, skinless chicken breasts, cut into 1-inch cubes

6 large russet potatoes, cut into ½-inch cubes

8 large carrots, peeled and cut into ½-inch-thick slices

1 cup uncooked long-grain rice

In the Dutch oven, mix together ketchup and cola until well combined. Stir in the chicken, potatoes, carrots, and rice. Cover with the lid and let simmer 60-90 minutes, using 10 coals underneath the oven, stirring occasionally. Replace coals as needed.

This is a thicker soup, so if you prefer a thinner base, gradually add water or chicken broth until desired consistency is reached.

Tip: To cook in a shorter amount of time, place 4 to 6 hot coals around the lid, but keep watch to make sure the soup stays at a constant simmer, not a boil.

HAMBURGER SOUP

1 (12-inch) Dutch oven, 30 hot coals plus extra if needed, cooking temperature 350 degrees

MAKES 12 TO 16 SERVINGS

1 pound ground beef

1 cup chopped onion

1 cup chopped green bell pepper

1 (29-ounce) can Italian stewed tomatoes, with liquid

1 (16-ounce) can tomato sauce

1 (15.25-ounce) can whole kernel corn, drained, optional

5 tablespoons Worcestershire sauce

2 teaspoons chili powder

1 teaspoon garlic powder

1 (32-ounce) can red beans, rinsed and drained

8 cups water

3 carrots, peeled and thinly sliced

3 russet potatoes, cut into 1-inch cubes

4 stalks celery, sliced

1 bay leaf

Brown beef, onion, and bell pepper in Dutch oven until beef is cooked through, using 30 coals underneath the oven. Drain excess grease and add tomatoes, tomato sauce, corn, if using, Worcestershire sauce, chili powder, onion powder, beans, water, carrots, potatoes, celery, and bay leaf; stir.

Bring to a boil, and then remove enough coals from underneath the oven to reduce heat to a low simmer. Cover with the lid and simmer for 60 minutes, stirring often. Replace coals as needed. Remove bay leaf before serving.

DUTCH OVEN STEW

1 (12-inch) Dutch oven, 24 hot coals plus extra if needed, cooking temperature 350 degrees

MAKES 10 TO 12 SERVINGS

1 pound lean beef stew meat

1 medium onion, chopped

2 (10.5-ounce) cans condensed cream of
   mushroom or chicken soup

1 to 2 soup cans of water

2 cups sliced celery

2 cups sliced carrots

6 potatoes, cut into cubes

1 (14.5-ounce) can whole kernel corn,
   with liquid

1 (14.5-ounce) can whole green beans,
   with liquid

Place stew meat in Dutch oven, cover with the lid, and brown, using 10 coals underneath the oven and 14 on top. Check often and stir so that the meat is evenly browned on all sides. Add onion, soup, and 1 can water for a thick stew or 2 cans water for a thinner stew. Stir well to combine. Add the celery, carrots, potatoes, corn, and beans.

Bring to a boil using 24 coals underneath the oven, and then remove enough coals to reduce to a low simmer. Cover with the lid and let simmer for 60 minutes, until carrots and potatoes are tender, stirring occasionally. Replace coals as needed.

WHITE CHILI

1 (12-inch) Dutch oven, 30-40 hot coals plus extra if needed, cooking temperature 350 degrees

MAKES 12 TO 14 SERVINGS

1 pound dry white beans

8 to 10 cups water, divided, plus enough to cover beans

4 tablespoons butter

1 medium onion, diced

4 tablespoons chicken bouillon granules

2 teaspoons salt, plus more to taste

2 (6.5-ounce) cans chunk chicken, drained

2 (4-ounce) cans diced green chiles

1 (16-ounce) container sour cream

Cilantro, for garnish, optional

Rinse and pick through beans, place in a large bowl, and cover with water; set aside until ready to use.

Melt butter in the Dutch oven, using 10 coals underneath the oven. Add onion and sauté until translucent. Drain the beans and add to the onion along with the bouillon, salt, and 8 cups water. Bring to a boil. Cover with the lid and cook for 2-3 hours, or until beans are tender, using 30 to 40 coals underneath the oven, stirring occasionally. Replace coals as needed. Check the water level often and add more if necessary.

Add the chicken and chiles, replace the lid, and cook for 30 minutes more. Stir in sour cream. Remove enough coals to reduce to a low simmer until ready to serve. Garnish with cilantro before serving, if desired.

Tip: In order to maintain the temperature of the beans when adding more water, make sure the water is as hot as possible.

DESSERTS

RASPBERRY-PEACH PIE

1 (12-inch) Dutch oven, 24-26 hot coals plus extra if needed, cooking temperature 350 degrees

MAKES 8 SERVINGS

Cooking spray

1 ½ cups sugar

7 tablespoons Clear Jel thickening starch

6 to 8 ripe peaches, peeled and sliced

2 cups fresh raspberries

2 teaspoons almond extract

½ cup red wine

2 cups shortening

4 cups flour

1 cup hot water

½ teaspoon salt

2 tablespoons butter, cubed

¼ cup milk

In a large mixing bowl, mix together the sugar and Clear Jel. Add the fruit, almond extract, and wine. Stir gently.

In a separate bowl, cut shortening into flour with a pastry cutter until it resembles coarse crumbs. Add water and salt and gently toss with a fork just enough to moisten. Knead dough until uniform in texture, and then divide into 2 balls. On a lightly floured surface, roll 1 of the dough balls out to a ¼-inch-thick circle, making sure it is large enough to completely cover the bottom of the Dutch oven and up the sides about 2 inches. Fold dough in half and gently place in bottom of Dutch oven that has been prepared with nonstick cooking spray.* Unfold dough, and press into the bottom and halfway up the sides of the oven. Carefully spoon the filling over the bottom.

Dot fruit filling with cubes of butter. Roll out second ball of dough for top crust, large enough to cover the filling. Place dough over filling and seal the bottom and top dough edges together with a little bit of water. Brush top crust with milk. Cut a few slits for venting. Brush top crust with milk. Cover with the lid and bake for 50-60 minutes, or until the crust turns golden and the filling is bubbling, using 10 coals underneath the oven and 14 to 16 on top. Replace coals as necessary.

*Tip: Cut 3 long strips of parchment paper and lay them across each other in a spoke-like pattern in the bottom and up the sides of the oven, pressing firmly in the corners. Cut a round piece of parchment to fit the bottom of the oven and lay it over the strips. The parchment strips will help you lift the pie out of the oven with ease. Make sure the pie is completely cooled before removing from the oven.

PECAN PIE

1 (10-inch) Dutch oven, 23 hot coals plus extra if needed, cooking temperature 400 degrees

MAKES 8 SERVINGS

Cooking spray

4 eggs

1 1/3 cups sugar

1 1/3 cups corn syrup*

4 tablespoons butter, melted

1 1/2 teaspoons vanilla extract

1 1/3 cups chopped pecans

1 (9-inch) refrigerated piecrust

In a large mixing bowl, beat eggs until well combined; add the sugar and mix well. Stir in the corn syrup. Add butter and vanilla and mix well. Stir in pecans.

Roll the pie dough out so that it is large enough, but not too thin, to press into the bottom and up the sides of Dutch oven that has been prepared with nonstick cooking spray or parchment paper (see Tip on page 107). Spoon filling over crust. Cover with the lid and bake for 65-75 minutes, or until a knife inserted into the center comes out with a clear, shiny coating, using 8 coals underneath the oven and 15 on top. Replace coals as needed.

*Note: Light corn syrup gives this pie a lighter taste and color, whereas dark corn syrup will give it a richer taste with a darker color.

CHERRY PIE

1 (12-inch) Dutch oven, 32–35 hot coals plus extra if needed, cooking temperature 400 degrees

MAKES 8 SERVINGS

Cooking spray

3 cups flour

3 ½ cups plus 1 ½ teaspoons sugar, divided

1 ½ teaspoons salt

¾ teaspoon baking powder

1 ½ cups shortening

¾ cup ice water

1 egg

2 tablespoons water

8 cups washed and pitted fresh pie cherries and any excess juice

2 teaspoons Fruit-Fresh Produce Protector

¾ cup Clear Jel thickening starch

2 teaspoons almond extract

In a large mixing bowl, mix together the flour, 1 ½ teaspoons sugar, salt, and baking powder. Cut shortening into the flour mixture with a pastry cutter until it resembles coarse crumbs. Slowly stir in the ice water until the mixture holds together and forms a dough. Roll out three-fourths of the dough on a lightly floured surface to a ¼-inch-thick circle, making sure it is large enough to completely cover the bottom of the Dutch oven and up the sides about 2 inches. Fold dough in half and gently place in bottom of chilled* Dutch oven that has been prepared with nonstick cooking spray or parchment paper (see Tip on page 107). Unfold dough, and press into the bottom and halfway up the sides of the oven.

In a small bowl, whisk together the egg and water, and brush the bottom dough with the egg wash. Place cherries in a large bowl. In a separate bowl, mix 3 ½ cups sugar, Fruit-Fresh, and Clear Jel together and pour over cherries. Slightly mash the cherries as you stir in the sugar mixture and add the almond extract. Spoon filling into bottom of Dutch oven.

Roll remaining dough out large enough to cover filling; seal the bottom and top dough edges together with water and form a decorative edge, if desired. Cut slits to vent top. Brush with remaining egg wash. Cover with the lid and bake for 60–80 minutes, or until crust turns golden and filling is bubbling, using 12 to 15 coals underneath the oven and 20 on top. Replace coals as necessary.

*Tip: To chill the Dutch oven prior to use, set it over a bag of ice.

APPLE SPICE CAKE

1 (12-inch) and 1 (10-inch) Dutch oven, 36 hot coals, cooking temperature 375 degrees

MAKES 12 SERVINGS

CAKE

1 (15.25-ounce) box spice cake mix

1 ¼ cups water

⅓ cup vegetable oil

3 egg whites

2 (21-ounce) cans apple pie filling

SAUCE

1 ½ cups light brown sugar

¾ cup light corn syrup

4 tablespoons butter

½ cup light cream

CAKE

In a large mixing bowl, combine cake mix, water, oil, and egg whites until thoroughly mixed; set aside.

Fit a piece of parchment paper in the bottom of the 12-inch Dutch oven. Pour pie filling over parchment paper and then pour the batter over pie filling.

Cover with the lid and bake for 25-35 minutes, or until a toothpick inserted in the center comes out clean, using 8 coals underneath the oven and 18 on top. Remove from Dutch oven by gently jiggling cake to loosen from the sides of the oven. Invert cake onto a cool, 12-inch Dutch oven lid and remove parchment paper.

SAUCE

In the 10-inch Dutch oven, heat the brown sugar, corn syrup, and butter over a low heat until mixture reaches a soft-ball stage, stirring occasionally, using 10 coals underneath the oven. Add the cream and heat for 2 minutes more. Serve cake with sauce drizzled over top.

CHOCOLATE-PEPPERMINT CAKE

1 (12-inch) Dutch oven, 24 hot coals, cooking temperature 350 degrees

MAKES 12 SERVINGS

CAKE

Cooking spray

3 cups sifted flour

1 teaspoon salt

2 teaspoons baking soda

4 heaping tablespoons cocoa

2 cups sugar

2 teaspoons vinegar

10 tablespoons butter, melted

¼ teaspoon peppermint extract

2 cups cold water

¾ cup semisweet chocolate chips

FROSTING

¼ teaspoon salt

¼ cup sugar

2 egg whites, beaten

¾ cup light corn syrup

1½ tablespoons vanilla extract

⅛ cup crushed peppermint candies

⅛ cup chocolate syrup

CAKE

In a large mixing bowl, sift together the flour, salt, baking soda, cocoa, and sugar; set aside. In a separate bowl, combine the vinegar, butter, peppermint extract, and water; mix well. Add to dry ingredients and stir until smooth; stir in chocolate chips. Pour batter into the Dutch oven that has been prepared with nonstick cooking spray containing flour. Cover with the lid and bake for 30 minutes, or until a toothpick inserted in the center comes out clean, using 10 coals underneath the oven and 14 on top. Let cake cool before removing from Dutch oven.

FROSTING

In a medium mixing bowl, gradually add salt and sugar to egg whites, beating until smooth. Slowly add corn syrup and beat until stiff peaks form; gently fold in the vanilla. Frost cooled cake and sprinkle candies over top. Drizzle chocolate syrup over individual servings.

LEMON-ORANGE CAKE

1 (12-inch) Dutch oven, 24 hot coals, cooking temperature 350 degrees

MAKES 12 SERVINGS

CAKE

Cooking spray

1 (15.25-ounce) box lemon cake mix

1 (3.4-ounce) box vanilla instant
  pudding mix

4 eggs

1/2 cup vegetable oil

1 cup water

GLAZE

2 teaspoons butter, melted

1/2 cup orange juice

1 orange zested, for garnish, optional

CAKE

In a large mixing bowl, combine cake mix, pudding mix, eggs, oil, and water; blend well. Pour batter into the Dutch oven that has been prepared with nonstick cooking spray containing flour. Cover with the lid and bake for 30–35 minutes, or until a toothpick inserted in the center comes out clean, using 10 coals underneath the oven and 14 on top. Let cake cool completely before removing from oven.

GLAZE

In a separate bowl, mix butter, orange juice, and powdered sugar together until smooth. If glaze is too runny, add more powdered sugar until desired consistency is achieved. Poke holes in the top of cooled cake using the handle of a wooden spoon and pour glaze over top. Garnish with orange zest, if desired. Let rest 10–15 minutes before serving.

BANANA CAKE

1 (12-inch) Dutch oven, 24 hot coals, cooking temperature 350 degrees

MAKES 12 SERVINGS

Cooking spray

²/₃ cup sugar

¹/₃ cup shortening

2 eggs

3 tablespoons buttermilk*

4 to 5 overripe bananas, mashed

2 cups flour

½ teaspoon baking soda

1 teaspoon baking powder

½ teaspoon salt

½ cup chocolate chips

In a large mixing bowl, cream the sugar and shortening together. Add the eggs, buttermilk, and bananas; stir well to combine. Mix in the flour, baking soda, baking powder, and salt until well blended and smooth. Add chocolate chips. Pour batter into the Dutch oven that has been prepared with nonstick cooking spray containing flour. Cover with the lid and bake for 35–40 minutes, or until a toothpick inserted in the center comes out clean, using 10 coals underneath the oven and 14 on top.

*Tip: Make your own buttermilk by combining 3 tablespoons milk with 1 teaspoon lemon juice.

CHOCOLATE CAKE

1 (12-inch) Camp Chef Ultimate Dutch Oven, 25 hot coals plus extra if needed, cooking temperature 350 degrees

MAKES 12 SERVINGS

CAKE

Cooking spray with flour

3 cups flour

1 cup plus 2 tablespoons cocoa powder

3 teaspoons baking soda

¾ teaspoon baking powder

¾ teaspoon salt

1 ¼ cups butter, softened

3 cups sugar

3 eggs

1 ½ teaspoons vanilla extract

1 ½ cups buttermilk (see tip on page 116)

1 cup plus 2 tablespoons sour cream

FROSTING

1 (8-ounce) package cream cheese, softened

2 tablespoons milk

¼ cup sugar

1 (12-ounce) container frozen whipped topping, thawed

1 (3.4-ounce) box instant chocolate pudding mix

CAKE

In a large mixing bowl, sift together the flour, cocoa, baking soda, baking powder, and salt; set aside. In a separate bowl, cream the butter and sugar together, and then beat in the eggs and vanilla. Alternately add buttermilk, sour cream, and flour mixture, stirring after each addition. Pour batter into the Dutch oven that has been prepared with nonstick cooking spray containing flour. Cover with the lid and bake for 70–80 minutes, or until a toothpick inserted in the center comes out clean, using 9 coals underneath the oven and 16 on top. Replace coals as needed. Let cake cool completely before removing from oven.

FROSTING

Mix together the cream cheese, milk, and sugar. Fold in whipped topping and pudding mix until thoroughly combined. Frost the cake when cooled.

RASPBERRY-PEACH COBBLER

1 (12-inch) Dutch oven, 24 hot coals, cooking temperature 350 degrees

MAKES 12 SERVINGS

1 (29-ounce) can peach slices or halves

1 (21-ounce) can raspberry pie filling, divided

1 (15.25-ounce) box yellow cake mix

Ice cream, for serving, optional

Drain juice from peaches and set aside. Place peach slices in the bottom of the Dutch oven, reserving 3 to 4 slices. Cut reserved slices into small pieces and place in a small bowl; stir in 4 teaspoons pie filling and set aside. Spoon remaining pie filling over peaches in bottom of oven.

In a large mixing bowl, make cake batter according to package directions, eliminating the eggs and using the reserved peach juice in place of water. If there isn't enough juice, add water to make up the difference. Stir the reserved peach and pie filling mixture into the batter and then evenly pour batter over the fruit in the bottom of the oven. Cover with the lid and bake for 30–35 minutes, or until the cake begins to pull away from the sides, using 10 coals underneath the oven and 14 on top. Serve warm and topped with ice cream, if desired.

SWEET POACHED PEARS

1 (12-inch) Dutch oven, 23 hot coals, cooking temperature 350 degrees

MAKES 6 SERVINGS

1 tablespoon butter

¼ cup ginger ale

25 caramels, unwrapped

25 cinnamon candies, such as Hot Tamales
   or Red Hots

1 (8-ounce) box Red Hots candies

6 ripe but firm pears, peeled

Heat the butter, ginger ale, caramels, and candies in warm Dutch oven, with 10 coals underneath, until caramels and candies have melted, stirring occasionally. Add more ginger ale as needed to cover the bottom of oven with poaching liquid ¼ inch deep.

Place pears in Dutch oven standing up. If pears are having a problem standing, slice a piece off the bottoms to make them more level. Cover with the lid and bake until fork-tender, using 10 coals underneath the oven and 13 on top. Baste pears with cooking sauce occasionally while they are cooking. When done, carefully remove pears and place on a cool serving platter. Drizzle cooking sauce over pears to serve.

WHITE CHOCOLATE CHEESECAKE

1 (10-inch) Dutch oven, 19 hot coals plus extra as needed, cooking temperature 325 degrees

MAKES 12 SERVINGS

7 whole graham crackers

¼ cup butter, cubed and softened

1 cup low-fat sour cream

4 eggs, separated into yolks and whites

½ cup sugar

1 tablespoon cornstarch

3 (8-ounce) packages low-fat cream cheese, softened

5 ounces white baking chocolate, melted

2 tablespoons lemon juice

2 tablespoons vanilla extract

2 tablespoons hot fudge ice cream topping

2 tablespoons caramel ice cream topping

½ cup chopped pecans

⅓ cup semisweet chocolate chips

Place graham crackers in a large zip-top bag, and crush to fine crumbs with a rolling pin. Add butter, seal bag, and mash together with your hands. Press crust mixture in the bottom and part way up the sides of the Dutch oven that has been lined with parchment paper (see Tip on page 107).

In a large mixing bowl, blend together the sour cream, egg yolks, sugar, cornstarch, cream cheese, white chocolate, lemon juice, and vanilla.

In a separate bowl, beat egg whites until stiff peaks form. Fold egg whites into cheesecake filling until combined. Pour filling over crust. Cover with the lid and bake for 45–60 minutes, or until center jiggles when lightly shaken, using 8 coals underneath the oven and 11 coals on top. Replace coals as needed. Remove from heat and let cool for 60 minutes. Carefully remove from oven with liner. Garnish with hot fudge, caramel, pecans, and chocolate chips.

STRAWBERRY TORTE

1 (10-inch) Dutch oven, 23-24 hot coals, cooking temperature 350 degrees

MAKES 10 SERVINGS

CAKE

Cooking spray

2 cups flour

½ cup vegetable oil

1⅓ cups sugar

1 cup milk

1¼ teaspoons baking powder

1 teaspoon vanilla extract

¾ teaspoon salt

2 eggs

FILLING

1¾ cups milk

1 (8-ounce) package cream cheese

1 (3.4-ounce) box instant vanilla
   pudding mix

1 teaspoon lemon zest

GLAZE

2 cups water

4 tablespoons cornstarch

1 envelope strawberry Kool-Aid

1 cup sugar

1 quart fresh strawberries, hulled and
   sliced

CAKE

In a large mixing bowl, add flour, vegetable oil, sugar, milk, baking powder, vanilla, salt, and eggs, and mix until well combined. Pour into the Dutch oven that has been prepared with nonstick cooking spray containing flour. Cover with the lid and bake for 30-35 minutes, or until a toothpick inserted in the center comes out clean, using 8 coals underneath the oven and 12 on top. Remove from heat and let cake cool completely before removing it from the oven.

FILLING

In a separate bowl, add ½ cup milk at a time to cream cheese, beating together until blended. Beat in pudding mix and lemon zest; refrigerate or place in a cooler until ready to use.

GLAZE

In a medium saucepan over 3 to 4 coals, bring the water, cornstarch, Kool-Aid, and sugar to a boil, stirring constantly, until thickened. Remove from heat and place in a bowl to cool. Cover with a lid or plastic wrap to prevent a skin from forming.

Using a paring knife, score a line around the outside of the cooled cake to use as a cutting guide. Cut horizontally through the center of the cake to make 2 layers using a serrated knife, or by sliding a string into the scored guide and pulling it through the cake.

Set the top half aside and spread a thin layer of glaze over the bottom half. Spread half the filling over the glaze and arrange half the strawberries evenly over top. Replace the top half of cake and spread remaining glaze in a 7-inch circle on top of cake. Use remaining filling to frame glaze, and place remaining strawberries on top.

INDEX

METRIC CONVERSION CHART

Volume Measurements		Weight Measurements		Temperature	
U.S.	Metric	U.S.	Metric	Fahrenheit	Celsius
1 teaspoon	5 ml	½ ounce	15 g	250	120
1 tablespoon	15 ml	1 ounce	30 g	300	150
¼ cup	60 ml	3 ounces	80 g	325	160
⅓ cup	80 ml	4 ounces	115 g	350	175
½ cup	125 ml	8 ounces	225 g	375	190
⅔ cup	160 ml	12 ounces	340 g	400	200
¾ cup	180 ml	1 pound	450 g	425	220
1 cup	250 ml	2¼ pounds	1 kg	450	230